OUR SMALLEST ALLY

A BRIEF ACCOUNT OF THE ASSYRIAN
NATION IN THE GREAT WAR

By

Rev. W. A. WIGRAM, D.D.

INTRODUCTION BY

GENERAL H. H. AUSTIN, C.M.G., ETC.

WITH A MAP

LONDON
SOCIETY FOR PROMOTING CHRISTIAN KNOWLEDGE
NEW YORK: THE MACMILLAN COMPANY
1920

Published in the United States 2010 by the Assyrian Academic Society
Email: info@aas.net
Website: www.aas.net

The special contents of this edition are copyright © 2010 by the Assyrian Academic Society. This edition is a reprint of the original edition published by the Society for Promoting Christian Knowledge, New York: The Macmillan Company, 1920.

All rights reserved. No part of this publication may be reproduced, stored in a retrieval system, or transmitted, in any form or by any means, electronic, mechanical, photocopying, recording, scanning or otherwise, without the prior permission in writing of the Assyrian Academic Society, or as expressly permitted by law.

You must not circulate this book in any other binding or cover and you must impose the same condition on any acquirer.

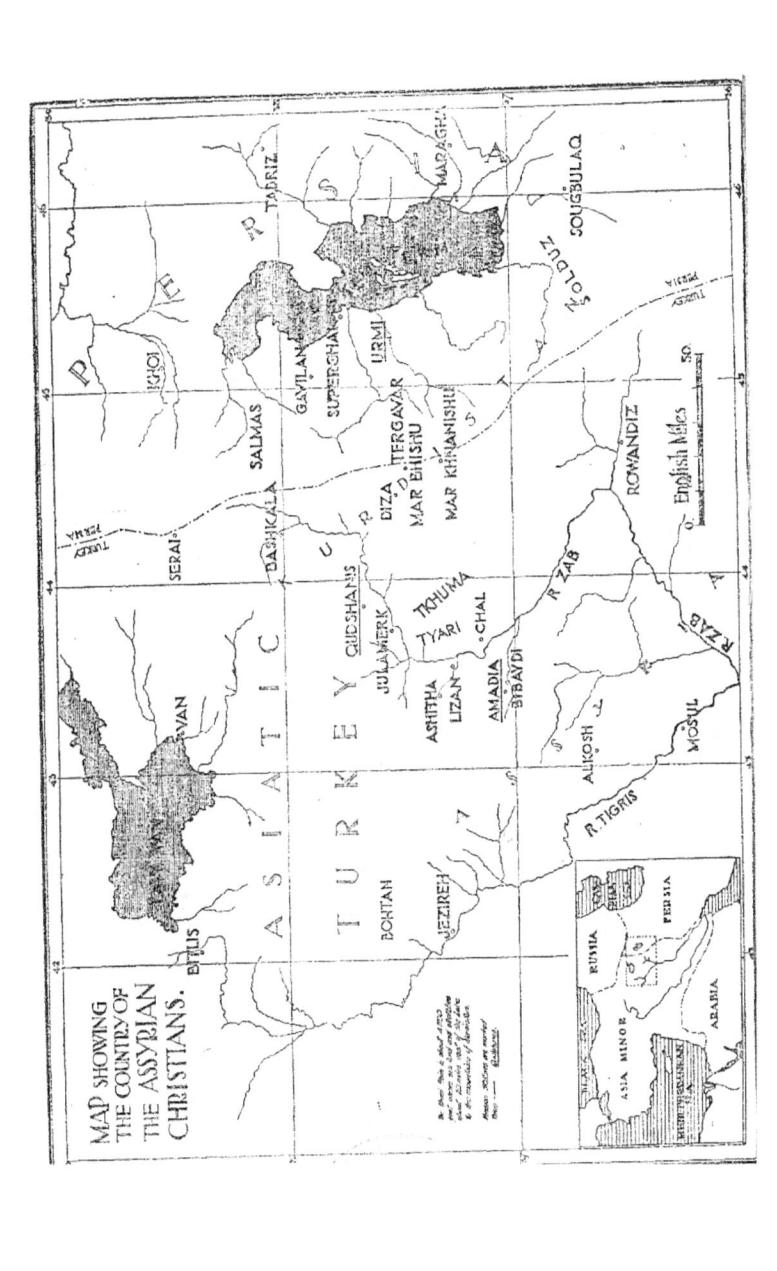

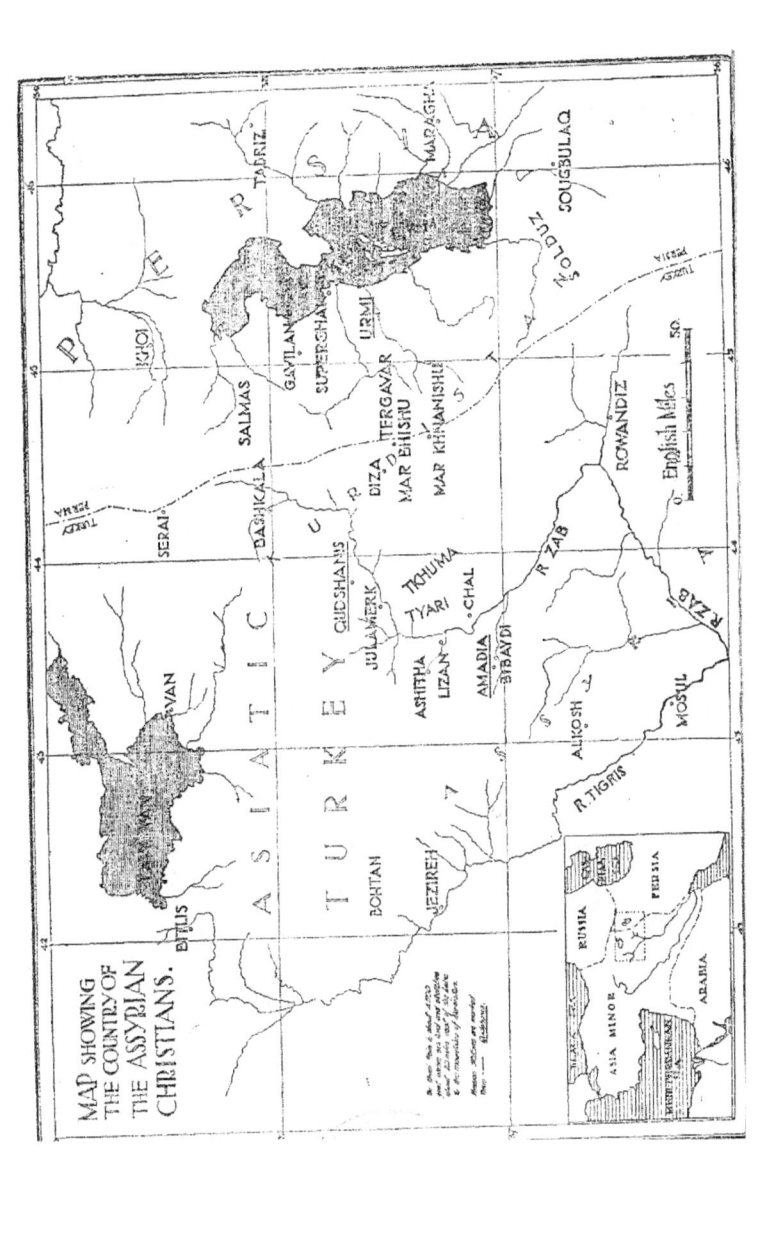

INTRODUCTORY LETTER

By BRIG-GEN. H. H. AUSTIN, C.M.G., C.B., etc.,
G.O.C. The Refugee Camp, Baqubah, Baghdad, 1918-1919.

I have been invited to write a brief introductory letter to Dr. Wigram's most interesting account of the part played by "Our Smallest Ally" in the Great War, and this I do with pleasure, as I feel that but few in England realize to what extent the small and obscure Assyrian nation helped to shoulder our burdens in the Middle East, by resisting the Turko-German aggression along the Turko-Persian frontier.

In the first place, Dr. Wigram needs no introduction from me, for his work, for more than a decade past, as a member of the Archbishop of Canterbury's mission to the Assyrians in Kurdistan and Urmi, is well known. His intimate knowledge of the country, the people, and the Syriac language places him in a unique position to deal with the subject that he has undertaken in his little pamphlet, while I can personally testify to the regard and affection in which he is held by the people whose sufferings and sacrifices he describes so graphically. It was whilst in command of the "Modern City of Refuge" at Baqubah, early in 1919, that I first had the pleasure of meeting Dr. Wigram. He then returned to Mesopotamia, after several years spent as a prisoner with the Turks in Asia Minor during the Great War, in order to place his services at the disposal of our Government in connection with the repatriation of the Assyrians – as was then hoped – to their former home. Although this hope has not yet been fulfilled, Dr. Wigram's assistance was of great value to me up to the time that I handed over the command to my successor, and we returned to England last summer. It was at Baqubah that Dr. Wigram collected the information that he now places before the public, and I think that all unbiased readers will admit, after a perusal of his pages, that "Our Smallest Ally" deserves well of the Entente nations for throwing in her lot with them, and thus sacrificing her little all in the cause of freedom.

I should here like to emphasize the point that the Assyrian mountaineers keenly felt that they had been deserted by the Russians, in the early days of the war, when they were left unaided to defend their homes against the Turks and Kurds, shortly after they had consented to fight for the Russians. Nevertheless, when these mountaineers reached their brethren in the plain of Urmi, and were again approached by the Russians, with the request that they would render assistance in Persia, they at once agreed to do so.

Two battalions of these mountaineers were organized and placed under the command of Russian officers, and became an integral part of the Russian army. Later, a third battalion was organized, under the special command of the Assyrian Patriarch. These battalions were on active service under Russian direction, and were utilized on expeditions against both Turks and Kurds, until the final dissolution of the Russian army. They then, up to July, 1918, formed part of the irregular force that defended the plains of Urmi and Salmas, and held the Turks in check on that frontier. In fourteen distinct engagements, from March to July, 1918, they defeated every Moslem force that was brought against them. Eventually, when their stock of ammunition was exhausted, and they were attached simultaneously by Turks, Kurds, and Persians, their position about Urmi became untenable, and the flight to Hamadan commenced. Subsequently, at Hamadan and Baqubah, an Assyrian contingent was raised from these mountaineer and plain refugees, and drilled and trained by British officers and N.C.O.s. The writer has recently heard, from officers commanding this mountain battalion, of the splendid work performed by his men, who were brigaded with Indian troops during recent operations against the truculent Kurds north of Mosul, in the year 1920.

Our Smallest Ally is now homeless, and dependent on our charity at Baqubah, for its lands and villages have been utterly destroyed, and it has the further mortification of seeing – from reasons beyond our control – that although it threw in its lot with the ultimately victorious side, Kurds, and others of the defeated enemy, are in practical possession of its ruined homesteads. Such a state of things is incomprehensible to the minds of this people, but it is due to the difficulties of the country, the entire absence of food in, and the inaccessibility of their homes, for purposes of ordinary transport, coupled with the extremely disorderly political conditions of Kurdistan and North-Western Persia.

These circumstances combine to render their safe re-instalment in their former lands, at present impracticable.

H. H. AUSTIN.
(Late G. O. C. Refugee Camp, Baqubah.)

February 6, 1920.

OUR SMALLEST ALLY

INTRODUCTION

In the following pages we make the attempt to narrate the fortunes of a curious Oriental nationality during the Great War.

This nation, which is known as the Chaldean or Assyrian "millet" (the technical Turkish term for a nation that is also a Church), may be said to have its centre at Mosul, so far as it has a centre at all; it extends thence as far as Baghdad in the south, while to the north-east its members are found as far as Urmi, over the Persian border; and to the north-west it reaches as far as Diarbekr. It must be understood, however, that it is only one of many national types in those lands, and by no means the dominant one. It is part of the problem of all the ancient Ottoman empire (a problem that the Europeans find it very difficult to grasp, let alone solve), that throughout its extent differing and often hostile nationalities are mixed together like dice in a bag.

The whole "millet" is Christian, having been so from very early ages, and its Christianity is of the type called "Nestorian", a name which evokes at once certain theological problems into which we need not enter now. It has its own hierarchy, with a "Patriarch" at the head of it, its own services, and its own Church history.

Naturally, it used the same scriptures and creed as other Christians, taking the Bible in the ancient Syriac translation known to scholars as the "Pshitta." The history of the Church up to the days of the rise of Islam in these lands has been fairly thoroughly studied by Western scholars, and perhaps we may refer English readers to a work called "An Introduction to the History of the Assyrian Church," written by the author of this book, and published by the S. P. C. K.

The story of the "millet" in medieval times is obscure, but it is known to have extended itself as far as Travancore in the south (and, indeed, representatives of it survive there to this day), and to the heart of China in the East. There at least one ancient monument, at Singan-fu, is a testimony to the missionary activity of this Church.

The body, originally one, has been much divided ecclesiastically, though some sense of ethnic unity underlies these divisions. Considerable portions submitted to Papal jurisdiction, and formed the "Chaldean Uniat" Church, under the Patriarch of that name, who has his throne at Mosul. Another portion became "Protestant" under the influence of American missionaries, who had their headquarters at Urmi in Persia. Those in this part of the world were also more or less under the influence of the Russian Orthodox Church, though it was a moot point how far this influence was political, and how far purely religious. In the mountains to the north of Mosul the people remained loyal to the ancient Church and hierarchy, and it is with this part of the nation that our narrative is principally concerned.

In these mountain districts the political position was strange and picturesque enough to merit description. The prevailing type of inhabitant was of Kurdish race (the plainsman being Arab by race and speech) and Turkish authority had never, practically speaking, extended itself into the district at all. The reason for this was simply the extremely rugged character of the land, where no made road exists, and no wheeled vehicle can possibly go. It had not been considered worth while to really subdue the province, and it had been left as "Ashiret" or "tribal;" under the rule, that is, of the local chiefs of the mountain tribes. The position was in fact not unlike that of the Scotch Highlands in the seventeenth century.

The government took what tribute it could get, when it could get it, and naturally assumed that it had full right to extend its authority in more regular fashion whenever it was convenient to do so. It even made sporadic efforts in that direction, now and then. The clans, large and small, recognised the overlordship of the Sultan in theory, reserving the right to disregard any particular order in fact. The country was a picturesque and disorderly Alsatia.

A fair proportion of these clans, and by no means the least wild among them, were Christian in religion. The only authority whom they recognised was their Patriarch, who claimed to be the real Patriarch of the whole "Chaldean" Church, though portions of it might have cast off his lawful jurisdiction. They paid their tribute through him – when they paid it – and regarded him as not only their spiritual head, but their temporal prince, or at least chief, as well. It is curious to note that here, as in Montenegro in the nineteenth century, temporal and spiritual headship were still combined, and were hereditary in one family, called that of "Mar Shimun." This was the official designation of the Patriarch.

The relations of these semi-independent Christian clansmen to their Kurdish neighbours were not more unfriendly than those of such clansmen usually are. Kurds and Moslems, but not fanatically inclined, and in "the days of our fathers" though feuds were pretty constant, they did not always follow the line of religious cleavage, and did not go very deep. "Grass soon grows over blood shed in fair battle," said a local proverb, and there were decent understandings as to what a gentleman might, and what he might not do, when he went out on the entirely laudable business of a raid against his neighbour!

Occasionally, indeed, the wars got far beyond this respectable level, and the great Raid if Bedru Khan Beg on the

Christians of Tiari in 1847, and the massacres that accompanied it, are remembered still. As a rule, however, things were far from intolerable. Weapons were even, each side was accustomed to see the other bear arms, and neither wanted to break away from a reasonable understanding. There was even a disposition in many Kurds to recognise the Patriarch of their Christian neighbours as the possessor of a sort of honorary religious precedency in all Kurdistan.

In the days of Abdul Hamid, however, i.e. from 1878 onwards, this changed for the worse, in many ways. That potentate was disposed to pet the Kurds at large, in the hope that they would be a support for his throne. He issued them arms, winked at their acts of oppression, and generally gave them cause to look on themselves as favourites. There was, in consequence, trouble all over the mountains, much raiding against which the Christians were given opportunity neither of redress nor of defence, and suffering for all. The Turkish revolution of 1908 gave promise of better things, but proved only a disappointment, for the Kurdish mal-practice was not stopped, and the only result of the change was the attempt to introduce that notorious plague, the Ottoman minor official, into districts where his corrupt personality had not intruded itself so far. To the old evils of a tribal state of things (from which the alleviations had been removed), there were added those of a corrupt civil service, with none of its advantages.

The people began to despair, then came the general break-up of the war, and we have now to chronicle what befell this nationality in that time of trial.

CHAPTER I

THE ASSYRIAN NATION IN THE GREAT WAR: MOUNTAIN FIGHTING

We wish to put on record a small episode of the great war; an episode wholly unimportant both politically and strategically, in that it was but a "side-show" to greater events; namely, the British expedition to Mesopotamia, and the Russian operations in trans-Caucasia and Armenia: events that were themselves no more than side-shows to the main drama of the colossal struggle. Yet this episode is nevertheless worthy of record, and that not only from the point of view of those who previously felt an interest in the fortunes of the tiny national and religious community concerned, but on account of its picturesque character, and for its deep human interest.

Elsewhere, the stage is so vast that it dwarfs all but a very few of the figures who appear on it, unless the view is purposely limited to some points of detail to the exclusion of all main questions; but here the relative smallness and unimportance of the theatre allow the characters to appear in something like their normal proportions.

The beginning of the war in August, 1914, meant for the Assyrians of the mountains of Kurdistan the beginning of a period of absolute isolation and suspense. The Patriarch, Mar Shimun, who had been summoned from Qudshanis (Kochanes) to Van on some government business, to confer with the Vali of that capital, returned with many promises of redress of all grievances, but with the expectation (justified both by experience and the event), that nothing would be done. The clouds grew steadily more black; a general massacre of all Christians was openly threatened, and actual massacres of Armenians (small in comparison with what was to happen later), were reported from all sides. There was fighting on the Turko-Persian border in districts of Tergawar and Margawar, between the turbulent local Christians and the Bagzade Kurds of that country, and at the beginning of November the expected happened, and Turkey actually entered the war. The event was immediately celebrated by free leave and licence being issued to the Kurds to sack the Christian villages of Albaq, near Bashkala, under the eyes of the Ottoman local authority.

The first fighting, however, took place in Persia, a country which the Turks had determined to regard (and that not altogether without excuse) as a Russian province. Regular Ottoman troops and Kurdish irregulars swept over the border, drove the Christian clans from Tergawar, and came down towards Urmi, intending to occupy that place and call on the Shiah Mussalman population to forget all feuds in Islam, and join with them in the Jehad which had been already proclaimed. There were Russian troops in Urmi, forming what was, in theory, a strong consular guard; and there were also, as now appeared, considerable stores of rifles, which were given out to the men of Tergawar, from whom it was possible to enrol two good fighting battalions; still, though these fought well, the odds in numbers were against them, and the invaders swept on till they were in actual occupation of Charbash, a Christian village barely a mile from the obsolete mud walls of Urmi town. In absolute confidence of victory, the Kurdish troops threw away their reserves of bread, being told by their officers, "You will not need them, for you will be eating fresh bread in Urmi tomorrow." In the event, however, the well-timed arrival of a small Russian reinforcement saved the situation; the expected attach proved a costly failure, and the Kurds were glad to get back to their hills before the winter set in, as usual, "between the Christmases" of 1914.[1]

Urmi considered itself as saved, particularly when the Russian column went down south to Saj Bulak to inflict a severe defeat upon a second Kurdish force at Dol, and clear that district also.

The Russian officers, however, were uneasy, having their eye on the general position in the Caucasus, and would not pledge themselves to a permanent occupation, saying to the American missionaries, "We can only promise that if we do have to evacuate, we will give you ample warning." This disappointment

---

[1] The Oriental Christmas falls thirteen days later than the European.

was followed by a staggering blow, for on the very day after the promise had been given, the amazed Americans found the whole Russian force in full retreat on Russia, leaving the people whom they had just rescued to the mercy of their enemies. To do the Russian general justice, the order was as great, and almost as unpleasant, a surprise to him as to the men of Urmi; for it came from the highest command, and was dictated by the very threatening state of things in Trans-Caucasia, where Enver Pasha, at the head of the main Turkish army, was threatening Batum. It is true that the danger was soon averted by the utter defeat of the Turkish invasion at Sara Kamish, but the fact was of no benefit to the Christians of Urmi. The Russians had gone, and did not intend to return for the time.

Panic ruled in the unhappy city. All Christians who were able to do so followed in the track of the retiring Russians and fled to Russia, about 10,000 finding safety in this way. The various mission yards, particularly the American, were crowded with refugees, and the attitude of the local Mussulmans soon became very threatening. There was, indeed, no general massacre, nor was there any second Kurdish invasion as yet. It is probable that the local magnates were by no means desirous to see either Turk or Kurd in their district. If, however, there was no general massacre there were plenty of small ones. On one occasion some sixty men were marched out of the city to the village of Gulpashin,[2] and there all put to death.

Among these martyrs was the Bishop, Mar Dinkha. Previously this man had been regarded in a serio-comic aspect at best. A Bishop who stopped when reading the service, to spell the next word; who brought a village rector – caught ploughing his glebe on Sunday – to a sense of the error of his ways by thrashing him with the pastoral staff till that symbol of office broke in two, could hardly be taken seriously.

But when that same man, crippled by brutal treatment, crawled from captive to captive in prison to administer spiritual consolation, he could be viewed in a new and more apostolic light. When we hear that at the last he stood encouraging each man who was led to death till his own turn came, we can put him on the level of some of his greatest fourth-century predecessors, and ask whether some Anglican prelates might not exchange their scholarship for that man's death.

There was another but rather smaller slaughter on the "hill of the Jews" in the village of Charbash. Worst of all, however, was the fate that befell some seventy Christians of Gawar, who had been forcibly impressed and brought down by the invading Turks to act as human baggage animals on their march, and left behind

---

[2] All were offered life on condition of acceptance of Islam. Two only accepted, and these both reverted afterwards and faced death for their faith.

on their precipitate retreat. These poor wretches were marched out by the local gendarmerie to the hill known as Kala Ismail Agha, several miles from Urmi, and there tied up in bunches and handed over to a gang of Kurds to be knifed or clubbed to death. Their bodies were left to the jackals, till such time as an American missionary (Mr. Allen) was able to give the bones decent burial.

In all of these horrors, the moving spirit was a local nobleman of education, Mejid es Sultaneh, who had in old days been distinguished as a friend of all foreigners, and to some extent as the protector of Christians, or at least of those who were his own feudal tenants. He had been accustomed to say (with perfect truth) that it was of no use to talk about reform in Persia until such time as the Shah had been persuaded to hang a Seyyid on every tree round Urmi, for those privileged "descendants of the prophet" were a standing obstacle to all improvement. In fact, some rather mis-timed zeal in this direction had brought about his exile, at which time he received great kindness both from British merchants and British officials. He was even allowed to take refuge at the British consulate at Tabriz. How it came about that a sojourn at Tiflis converted a rather free-thinking Anglophil into a pan-Islamic fanatic, we do not profess to explain, but such was undoubtedly the fact. Generally, the winter of 1914-1915 was a black one in Urmi.

In the mountains the case was different, for here the Turks were really anxious to avoid trouble with the Christians for the moment. The disaster of Sara Kamish had put a stop to all ideas of an invasion of Russian territory, and a Russian advance on Van and Erzerum was at least probable. If that should take place, the position of the mountain Assyrians on the flank of such an advance was important, and there were political reasons for gaining their loyalty as well. The Armenian massacres were now in full swing, and the presence of the American missionaries in the land made it impossible to conceal them altogether. The Turks were resolved to continue them (Talaat, then Minister of the Interior, and later Grand Vizir, had declared that he meant to "settle this Armenian question for the next fifty years at least"), but the policy needed concealment and apology, and it would be an obvious advantage to be able to say, "Here is a Christian millet that has such confidence in our justice, that it has thrown its lot in with us in this war of its own accord." Hence very high bids were made for what the Turks called Assyrian loyalty, and the Assyrians, with their old ideas of a shadowy independence, called alliance. They were to have absolute freedom for education, were to be given good guns, with salaries for their Patriarch, for all their bishops, and for their mountain chiefs. Promises, in fact, were cheap, and the Turk was lavish of them; and there is no doubt that a party in the nation were desirous of accepting them. They could argue, with perfect truth, that the adherence of so small a nation to the cause of the Entente could make no difference to them; and that they themselves, placed as they were absolutely in the jaws of the wolf, would never be blamed for making terms for themselves in the time of peril. Thus for a time things were in suspense. There was no fighting, but a good deal of dread of the future; and as a precaution the patriarchal family, and later the Patriarch himself, left the isolated village of Qudshanis, and went down to the Ashiret district of Diz, and to the relative safety of its rugged mountains.

In the spring of 1915, events forced the momentous decision on the nation; the Russian advance commenced, and what was left of the city of Van fell into their hands. It was a town of ruins; for it had been the scene of desperate fighting between the Armenian Tashnakists and the government troops, and the theatre of some of the most awful massacres of that awful time. The great American mission, among other buildings, had been destroyed. Now, however, in April, it fell into Russian hands, and the conquerors sent down a deputation to Bashkala and Julamerk, calling on the mountaineers to rise and fight for the Christians against the Mussalmans who had proclaimed the general "Jehad." At about the same time the Russians re-occupied Urmi, where peace and amnesty was proclaimed, and a time of relative safety began for all the inhabitants. The men of the mountains had now to make their definite choice.

A meeting of all the notables of the nation was held in Diz, and the matter was fully and anxiously debated; on the one side there could be argued the promises of the Turk, and the certainty of forgiveness by the English if the nation should elect to "plan for safety." On the other there was undoubtedly the feeling that they were now being asked to play their part in the general quarrel of all Christendom, and the fact that it was very doubtful whether the Turk either could or would keep his promises, or defend them from the Kurd in the mean time. Ultimately, on receiving Russian promises of support, they decided for the nobler and more dangerous of the alternatives; they definitely threw in their lot with the Entente against Turkey, and the nation was called to arms on the 10th May, 1915. A definite and formal declaration of war was sent by the heads of the nation to the Vali of Var. They were committed; and as soon as they were thus definitely committed; the Russians withdrew to Van and left their mountain allies to fend for themselves in the peril that they had now called upon to face on their behalf.

That peril became real at once. Qudshanis was attached and burnt by the Kurds, the patriarchal library and the English mission house sharing the common lot. Even the church books which had been concealed in what was held a safe place, were found and destroyed. The Turkish authorities had not lost all hope of winning over the mountaineers, and the Kaimmakam of Julamerk, Rajib Raghab Bey, sent frequent messages to the Patriarch at Diz. These, however, were all fruitless, and the spirits of the mountaineers rose to meet the danger; Shamasha[3] Ephraim's war song, written about this time, expresses their feelings, and it was chanted from village to village among the hills.

---

[3] I.e., "Deacon." The priests are not supposed to fight, but the deacons do.

ASSYRIAN WAR SONG
(By Shamasha Ephraim of Serai D'Mamidai, Van)

Brothers, up; arouse ye; shake off sloth and slumber!
Take each man his rifle for the battle with the Turk.
Now the day is dawning when we face our foemen.
Forth we go to battle in thy name, O Mar Shimun.

Rouse ye chiefs and princes, Maliks God-appointed;
Forward goes our army through the land we owned of yore.
Hear the rifle rattle echo from our mountains.
Forth we go to battle in thy name, O Mar Shimun.

Up, I say, ye captains; up, I say, ye Maliks!
Kings we had in olden time right mighty men of war.
Take we gun and powder; days of stress are on us.
Forth we go to battle in thy name, O Mar Shimun.

Lady of the Holy House, Surma stands amongst us;
Giver of high counsel to her brothers from a child.
"Now the very babe must bear the bow and arrows."
Forth we go to battle in thy name, O Mar Shimun.

Young men of the Nation, Clans renowned in story,
Stand by one another now in brotherhood and zeal.
Shall beloved Kochanes be a prey to foemen?
Forth we go to battle in thy name, O Mar Shimun.

Young men of the Nation, bide a band of brothers,
Tiari fast by Jilu and Tkhoma fast by Baz.
Listen to the roll of battle drums ye warriors.
Forth we go to battle in thy name, O Mar Shimun.

David is our leader, valiant in the combat;
He shall be our captain and set us in array!
He shall go before like sun and moon to guide us.
Forth we go to battle in thy name, O Mar Shimun.

Forth we go to battle, raging o'er the mountains;
Hearts all yearning forward to Mosul's fertile plains.
Nineveh's fair city summons back her children.
Forth we go to battle in thy name, O Mar Shimun.

On the Tigris' banks lies Nineveh the holy;
Her old walls shall be to us a diadem and crown.
There alone, Assyrians, can our race be established.
Forth we go to battle in thy name, O Mar Shimun.

Hark, our Nation calls – our great Assyrian mother;
Hark, young men, she calls you – calls each one of you by name.
Blest that youth for ever who will hear my calling.
Forth we go to battle in thy name, O Mar Shimun.

Now began a period of fighting that was desultory, but for all that severe, in the mountain districts, where the Assyrians, who could get no help except a few rifles and cartridges from their Russian allies, stood at bay among their crags and gorges against largely superior forces of Kurds and of regular Turkish troops from Mosul. The decision had been taken at the middle of May, and before the end of June the Berwar Kurds, with the garrison of Mosul to back them, had begun an organised attack on the Lizan valley of lower Tiari, while the Artosh Kurds, led by the Kaimakam of Julamerk, were threatening Chumba; and on the other side of the Zab the Agha of Chal had brought his forces against Salabekan and Tkhuma, and Sutu of Oramar, old enemy of the Assyrians, was taking the field against Jilu and Baz.

On the whole, this formidable series of attacks failed, or at least met with only partial success. The Lizan valley was occupied, with the village of Ashitha, but the attacks on Chumba d'Malik, Jilu and Salabekan were repulsed with heavy loss. When the onset was renewed some five days later, there was severe fighting at Mar Sawa, on the Zab. The bridge at that point was taken, retaken by the Christians, and finally taken and held by the Kurds; still they were never able to improve their success at this point and cross the Zab.

Broadly, the result of a week of severe fighting was, that the Assyrians lost the districts on the right or western bank of the

Zab, but were able to destroy the bridges and maintain their positions on the other bank. There was a pause after these first actions, and Mar Shimun employed it in a hurried visit to Diza in Gawar, where he could get into touch with the Russians in Van and Urmi, and ask urgently for help from both parties. This effort brought him plenty of congratulations and abundant promises, and a small but welcome supply of rifles and ammunition; but nothing more substantial than that.

Foiled, on the whole, in the open fighting, Haidar Beg Vali of Mosul, now sought to bring about the Assyrian surrender in a singularly dastardly fashion. Hormizd, the brother of Mar Shimun, was a prisoner in his hands. This young man had been in Constantinople for his education for two years before the war, and had been arrested and imprisoned there as soon as Turkey entered the struggle, so that there could be no political charge against him personally. He was now sent to Mosul,[4] and Haidar sent the following message to Mar Shimun: "Your brother is in my hands, and unless you and your nation will lay down your arms, that brother shall die." It was a terrible choice to have to make, and those who know the relations which existed between those two young men can understand the feeling with which Mar Shimun sent an answer which approached the heroic in its ring:

---

[4] Hormizd was arrested in Constantinople, and sent thence "to Mosul," but it is not certain that he ever reached that place.

"My people are my charge, and they are many. How can I give them up for the sake of one, even if that one be my own brother?" Hormizd was put to death, a martyr for the sake of his people; his death being as foul a judicial murder as any in the dark annals of the Turk.

Another appeal to the Russians in the month of August may have produced some small effect, if we can date there an episode which certainly occurred, though our informants were, in oriental fashion, clearer on details than on dates. A detachment of about 400 Cossacks seems to have been sent up from Urmi to the mountains, but its commander was either very rash, or very ignorant of the local conditions, for he allowed himself to become the guest of Sutu, the Agha of Oramar, and accepted guides from him, to conduct him through the mountain passes. Sutu, who entertained the detachment as his honoured guests, and kept some eighteen of them in his own house when the others departed, sent them off by the road to Neri, sending word at the same time to Sheikh Seyyid Mahommed (a relative of the Sheikh of Shamsdin), to the effect that the Russians were coming by the "Galia Balanda" (the "Deep Gorge"), and that if Mahommed would collect his men and attack them at that critical point, Sutu would have his own clansmen in their rear, to cut off all retreat.

This treacherous plan was executed, under the guidance of the two elder sons of Sutu, Osman and Tili, and the detachment cut off to the last man. The eighteen men left in the house of Sutu were also attacked and massacred, though one feels some satisfaction in recording that the crime was not completed without a fight, in which a son of Sutu was killed, and that arch-traitor himself wounded.

However, the Russian attempt to send help (if it was made at this time) thus failed completely, and the mountaineers were left to face the second attack of their enemies.

This was delivered in August, 1915, and on this occasion the invaders had the formidable help of the Barzan Kurds, a clan whose members seemingly had forgotten how the Christian Ashirets helped their former chief, Sheikh Selim, in the days when he was a fugitive from the Turk, and had forgotten too the execution of that beloved chieftain of theirs by the Ottoman government in the early days of the war. Delivered from the south (the vulnerable line), this attack succeeded, and Tkhoma, Tiari, Jilu and Baz were ravaged pitilessly. As usual in a "Jehad," all the usual courtesies of tribal war were neglected, for it is understood that when you go to war in the name of Allah you may commit any atrocity that you please. Houses were burned, water-channels (which in these mountains have to be carried in poplar-trunks along precipitous rock faces), were broken down, churches by the score were desecrated and plundered. Some forty churches in Jilu alone met this fate, though it is to be hoped that the Kurds, with characteristic laziness, refrained from serious injury to their very solid fabrics. This point will have to be examined later, and it must be owned that the fact that the Turks had provided the Turks with bombs for the mountain fighting opens a disquieting possibility.

It was at this time that the famous church of Mar Zeia in Jilu was plundered for the first time in its history, and a collection of votive curios that was absolutely unique was scattered to the winds. Hitherto it had been guarded by its most precious possession, a firman of protection which was at least believed to be an autograph letter of the Prophet himself, written on linen; and which had been sufficient shield for the shrine even in the days of Bedr Khan Beg and his great ravagings. Now, however, even that failed; the letter was carried off as a sacred prize, and the Church itself was looted. The seventh-century jars, brought from China by Nestorian missionaries in old days, were smashed by savages who did not know that their German allies would gladly have bought them at their weight in gold; and the *ex voto* offerings of centuries, which had given that church the look of a wild museum, were wantonly destroyed. The church, however, was not quite unavenged in its ruin. A certain fanatical young Kurdish Agha, eldest son of Simco, Agha of the Shekak Kurds (whom we shall meet again in the course of this narrative), was the leader of the spoilers, proclaiming like "fanatic Brooke" at Lichfield that he hoped to see the downfall of every Christian church in the land. As he stood at the church door superintending the removal of the plunder, a shot fired at extreme range took him in the head, and he fell in front of the church that he was desecrating.

Though thus beaten from their valleys, the men of the nation had not lost hope as yet, and were still unbroken in spirit. They fell back upon the "yailas," the summer pastures whither the sheep are always driven in the heats; and though the Kurds attacked these refuges again and again, they were always beaten back, and sallying parties were even able to venture down into the villages and bring back some small stores of corn. The Christians had food for a while, for the flocks were with them still, and water was abundant in that land where the snowdrifts never melt altogether. The lack of salt, however, was severely felt, and brought positive illness, as well as that utter distaste for all food which, in an Oriental, often means a lack of interest in life and surrender to the coming of death.

The Patriarch shared all his people's privations, and indeed suffered more than they did, for by the custom of their fathers he was forbidden to eat meat, which was the only provision that was to be had in any abundance, and he and other "rabbans" seem to have lived for a long time on milk and parched corn.

If, however, the position on the "yailas" could be defended against open attack, it was clear to all that it would soon become untenable for other reasons. It was now late in September of the year 1915, and with the first snows of winter (which often fall in October at the altitude of 10,000 feet at which the nation was encamped), human life would become impossible on the heights. It was resolved to make a last appeal for Russian help, and with that object Mar Shimun, accompanied by Khoshaba of Lizan and two other companions, started on the dangerous journey that was to take them through the leaguer of the Kurds and down to Persian territory. The Patriarch was at this time, with the mass of his people, on the table-land of Shina, at the headwaters of the Tal and Tkhuma gorges; and the enemy held all the country between him and Urmi, particularly the district of Gawar, where Nuri Beg had just carried out a specially cruel massacre of the unarmed Christian population of the plain. Still, it was felt that the attempt had to be made, however slender its chances of success, and travelling by night with experienced guides, the little party accomplished their daring journey in safety and arrived in the district of Salmas. The local Russian officers, however, declared that they were in no position to do anything, and could only urge the Patriarch, now that he had himself escaped, to remain in the safety which he had attained, and not to sacrifice his own life. This (be it recorded to his honour) was a course that he would not hear of, and without waiting even one night in the camp of the

Russians, he went back to the mountains to share the fate of his nation.

He and his advisers had now to face the fearful problem, by what possible means a crowd of some twenty-five thousand men, women and children, with a mass of flocks in addition, could be extricated from the plateau on which they were invested by the enemy, and marched down to safety. The country, as all know who have had to traverse it, is one of the most rugged in the world; the men were not soldiers, but undisciplined tribesmen, few of whom could ever rise to any conception of duty to a larger entity than their own clan. Still, if the attempt was probable destruction, to remain for the winter was certain death, and under this spur the plan was formed. The bulk of the Kurds were to the east of them, guarding the direct road to Persia, and drawing their food from the fertile plain of Gawar. It was determined to go in the opposite direction, marching with all possible speed down the two valleys of Diz and Tal, to cross the Zab by the two bridges at or near the foot of those gorges, and break them down as soon as the crossing was done. The two columns could then unite in the district of Berwar, north of Qudshanis, one day's long march from the district of Albaq, where Russian support might be hoped for at last. The plan was attempted, and in the face of all military probability, was actually carried out with success. If the Christians were undisciplined clans, the Kurds were little better, and when they found the "yaila" of Shina had been abandoned, they stayed to quarrel over the flocks that had been left upon it, and the migrating nation of Christians were able to effect the crossing of the unfordable Zab and break the bridges behind them. Only small bands of Kurds persisted in the pursuit, though these were able to harass the march seriously.

Mar Shimun himself was with the party that marched by Tal, and the route necessarily took him by a pass where for the last time he and his could look down the slopes to where the village of Qudshanis lies upon its sloping "alp." It was then that he broke out with the one word of complaint that was known to fall from him in the war, and exclaimed, "When shall I ever drink the water of Qudshanis again?" The words prompted an incident which is none the less genuine for being an exact parallel to an episode in the life of David; for the circumstances were roughly parallel, and both leaders had, whatever their failings, that personal charm that made the wild men whom they ruled ready to risk life to gratify even the lightest wish of their chief. Some young men who had heard the words started out at once with a "talma," or water-jar, and breaking through the lines of the pursuing Kurds, reached the stream that flows down to Qudshanis, and brought the water to their chieftain. To make the parallel quite complete, he should have refused to drink of what had become the blood of heroes, and poured it out in sacrifice; this piece of ritual, however, was not in accord with Nestorian habits, and we believe that he merely drank it with warm thanks to those who brought the gift.

The junction with the Diz column of Assyrians was duly effected at Kotranis in Berwar, and the march on Albaq resumed; still, the retiring army were not clear of their enemies, for the Kurds had made their way across the Zab by a higher bridge – probably the curious natural bridge of Hezekian – and barred the retreat to safety. There was a last sharp action in the hills, in which Khoshaba[5] of Lizan particularly distinguished himself, and the defeat of the Kurds opened the way to the comparative safety of the district of Albaq, whence the emigrants could gradually make their way over an easy pass to the Persian district of Salmas. It was not a routed force that arrived, nor had these men of the mountains any cause to be ashamed of their record.

They had deliberately, and in the face of great temptation and danger, thrown in their lot with what they believed to be the right; they had seen themselves abandoned by those who had urged them to this course, and yet had stood by it, and defended themselves against tremendous odds in a very creditable way. Though beaten from their country at last, they were no more crushed than were the Serbs in like case, but conducted an orderly retreat in the face of immense difficulties, and brought

---

[5] I.e., "Sunday," a common name among the Assyrians, as Domingo is among the Spaniards.

them down with not only their women, but their flocks and herds as well. So, arrived in Persia, they remained there, ready for the next turn of fortune's wheel.

CHAPTER II

IN THE PLAINS OF PERSIA

To say that the state of things in Urmi was anomalous, at the time that the mountain Assyrians poured down into the district, is to understate the case. In theory Persia was, of course, an independent and neutral power, whose territory all combatants were bound to respect. As a matter of fact, it was ruled by a government far too feeble in strength to enforce neutrality, and far too feeble in mind to take a side in the struggle. Further, both parties were so anxious to get a "Mussalman power" to declare openly for them, that they were extremely unwilling to declare open war upon her; while both found themselves quite unable to avoid treating her territory in the most cavalier fashion. Before the war, Urmi had been in fact the position of a small Russian garrison and arsenal; and the first act of the war had been a Turkish invasion of the district, that had been repelled by the Russians and by some Persian subjects, but emphatically not by the Persian Government. Now, it was still, in theory, an important provincial town in Persia, ruled by a governor nominated by the Prince of Azerbaijan – who is always the heir-apparent of Persia – and this governor was, as always, in the town, ruling and taking counsel with the Mussalman notables of the place. But there was also in the town a Russian consul, and a very considerable garrison which were under his orders; and this official took counsel, not with the Mussalmans, but with the "Mutwa" (council) of the Assyrians of the town, a body entirely unknown officially to the Persian Governor. Having thus taken counsel, the Russian would issue his directions to the Governor, who usually found it advisable to carry them out. Now this state of things was, to put it mildly, displeasing to a set of extremely fanatical Shiah Moslems, all of whom could look back to days when Christians were in a proper state of subjection, and had to get off their donkeys and stand at the salute when the Moslem rode past on his horse. Now it was the Christians who rode the horses, thanks to the wealth they had acquired by trade, and the backing of the "yellow dogs" from Russia; and to tell the truth some of them were swaggering as only the oriental who has the upper hand can swagger, and not at all disinclined to make the most of their advantage over those who had, most unreasonably, looked down upon them in the past. Equality is a thing that no oriental can comprehend. The rule of one man, or caste, over all others, is the natural thing, and why should you seek rule, if not for the rewards of ruling?

The situation then was already full enough of possibilities of trouble, when it was further complicated by the arrival of 20,000 mountaineers, men who had lost their all, and were accustomed to look on raid and robbery as ordinary incidents of life, and whom the plainsmen were accustomed to think of as a sort of contemptible but yet formidable savage, not to say demon.

Yet at first these mountaineers – to quote an American missionary of great experience[6] - "behaved very much better than might reasonably have been expected of them." It is true that they were a hard handful to control and plundered a good deal; this was particularly the case round about Urmi itself – where it mattered most, of course – for there no authority was present to control them. Those who remained in the district of Salmas, or Salamast, which is about one day to the north of the city, were under the direct eye of their Patriarch, and there were no complaints made against them. On the other hand, it may be urged that many of the Urmi folk, both Moslem and Christian, if they found trouble, were asking for it rather emphatically. When twenty thousand hungry men are thrown upon you by the chances of war, if you do not help them they will most certainly help themselves, no matter what their race, colour or religion; in this case many of the men of the plain seemed disposed only to make as much as might be out of their visitors, and would only sell food at high prices, or even insist on the surrender of guns in exchange for it. When that line is taken with starving, armed, and

---

[6] Dr. McDowell, whose work as relief administrator in these times of trouble was beyond praise.

undisciplined men in a land of plenty, the probable consequences are pretty plain to see.

Further, the mountaineers had even more serious things to complain of. We said that there was always a Persian governor in Urmi, and the action taken by one of the holders of this office is worthy of record, as showing how mere fright will often urge an oriental into horrible acts of cruelty.

His Excellency, the Governor, who was a member of the Royal House of Persia, was proceeding from Tabriz to Urmi to take up his post, to which he had been newly appointed, with an escort of about three hundred cavalry. Passing round the northern end of Lake Urmi, he reached a point known as "Snatchbeard Corner," where the road turns so abruptly round a nose of rock that it is said that a highwayman can catch his victim by the beard before he can be seen. Here he found a party of two hundred mountaineers, peaceably sitting by the roadside, who saluted him as he drove past.

Without the least provocation, and simply from the general state of pure panic that made him see a murderer in every mountaineer, he turned his escort loose upon them, and allowed these soldiers to massacre, pillage, and outrage as they liked while he sat in the carriage and looked on.

We may add a word on the conclusion of this gentleman's career in the city of Urmi. When the Russians finally departed from that city there was an *emeute,* in the course of which the bazaar was burned. On this occasion his Highness the Governor left his post and fled for refuge to the American mission, where he begged for admittance and protection, literally with tears. He was not admitted, but the son of one of the missionaries, a lad of seventeen, agreed to go back with him to the Government Serai; and there the youth consented, at the Governor's prayer, to stay with him, and this scion of Persian royalty actually sat for hours holding the American boy's hand, like a frightened child in a thunderstorm, till the riot was over!

The mountaineers were not idle during their stay in the plain, for they were able to conduct a series of well-arranged raids against the Kurds of their own country, turning out Chal and Oramar, besides beating up the summer quarters of the nomad Hereki and acquiring quite a lot of sheep as their reward. The sack of the stronghold of Sutu Agha, at Oramar, gave them back quite a fair percentage of the plunder taken from the villages of Jilu, and when Chal fell into their hands for the moment – during a well-planned raid under the leadership of David, brother of the Patriarch – the son of Agha was himself among the prisoners. Here, however, a pleasing touch of chivalry on either side lightened a rather sombre story, for the young fellow was released by his captors, on the sole condition that he should do his best to bring about an exchange of prisoners, man for man. This agreement was carried out loyally, and the Assyrians effected an unmolested retreat.

Indeed, the feuds and battles between Assyrian and Kurd in pre-war days in the mountains were conducted, as a rule, with little rancour and a keen sense of sport. The combatants are men of much the same type, and to some extent of the same blood, though probably neither side would admit the truth of that statement.[7] It is only where treachery has been used, or the rules of the game broken otherwise, that a real "blood feud" as distinct from an ordinary tribal quarrel, is handed on from year to year, or at times, from father to son. Speaking normally, the proverb quoted above holds good, and "grass soon grows over blood shed in fair fight"; there is hope for the future of the mountain districts in this fact.

Broadly, there was an informal truce in the Urmi district, from the January of 1916 until the end of the following year. The district was, in fact, though not in theory, a self-governing province in Persia; and the Mussalmans submitted to what was practically Russian control. The Persian Governor accepted the orders of the Russian consul, and the small Russian force present in the city was gradually augmented. The Russians sent a fair supply of rifles and ammunition, and a very large number of decorations,

---

[7] Some "Kurds" are lapsed Christians; some Christians probably Kurdish by descent, also there are occasional marriages by capture.

which were prized almost as highly and worn universally. The personal congratulations of the Tsar were sent to Mar Shimun, who visited Tiflis to receive high decorations from the Grand Duke Nicholas himself. The whole position was entirely outside all international law and order, and as completely outside the legal theory of things in Persia; still, on the whole, the Assyrian nation was holding its own and existing as a corporate body politic in the land, and it continued to do so until the autumn of 1917, when the unmistakable signs of complete collapse began to show themselves in Russia, and aroused well-grounded anxiety.

Meantime, the Russian breakdown had naturally been attracting attention elsewhere, and attempts were being made to buttress that falling wall. A Franco-British military mission had been despatched to the Caucasus; and all the material of a large army, provided by British and French arsenals, had been sent to that district, in preparation for a great blow on the Turk from that direction.

The position of the Assyrians in Urmi was known, of course, to the authorities of this mission, and plans were formed by which their services could be utilised as part of a great line of defence, extending from the Black Sea to the Persian Gulf, that was to block the known German designs on India. General Offley Shore's idea was that common action might be arranged between the Armenians of Van, the Assyrians in Urmi, and a Kurdish chief whose territory consisted of the range of mountains separating those two lake basins, viz., Simco, Agha of the Shekak Kurds.

Simco, to give him the name by which he is generally known – though this is actually a Kurdish contraction of Ismail – was the leader of a tribe of about two thousand mounted men. He was – or had been – a colonel of Hamidie in the Turkish service, but was believed to be open to argument on that point, in that he was really only a fervent worshipper of the rising sun. There was reason to think that he was resolutely anti-Persian in his politics; for his elder brother and predecessor in the chieftainship, Jaffar Agha, had been murdered with every possible aggravation of treachery and post-mortem insult by the late Shah of Persia, at a time when that worthy, as heir-apparent (Vali-ahd) was Governor of Azerbaijan. Simco had then declared that he would never trust a Persian, or look on one as a gentleman, again. He had been the friendly host of British consuls on more than one occasion – though he sometimes gave them no choice as to whether they would accept his hospitality or no; and had once carried friendship so far as to offer to exchange his latest married wife against a Mannlicher rifle owned by a British officer.[8]

Altogether, General Shore thought that he was a man who might be won, and who was worth winning from his position and power. The Armenian commander in Van, Hanpartsunian,

---

[8] Capt. Dickson, R.A., then British Military Consul at Van.

thought differently, and had the deepest suspicion of the Kurd's good faith; but he was over-ruled by the General, and two officers in the British Intelligence Service, Captain Gracey and Lieut. McDowell, were despatched to Simco's stronghold at Chara to enter into a league with him. Simco was more than ready to agree, and swore on the Koran to fight for English, Kurds and Armenians in fellowship with Mar Shimun, whom he declared that he regarded as honorary head of Kurdistan. Mar Shimun on hearing of the scheme agreed to fall in with it, though he admitted to Captain Gracey that he shared the Armenian leader's doubts as to Simco's honesty. "Well," said that officer, "you probably would do well not to trust him too far; but if you and the Armenians work together, then you have him between the jaws of your pincers, and he can do little harm." Actually, the suspicions were more than justified, for loyalty and honour were things unknown to the Kurd, who had been given a most exaggerated idea of his own importance by a rather ill-timed visit of some French officers after the agreement had been made by Gracey, and who was quite ready to deal with Persian or Turk if that seemed likely to pay him best. However, the agreement was made, and Capt. Gracey went on to Urmi to make arrangements with the Assyrian nation at that point.

A great meeting was held for this purpose in the American Mission premises, under the presidency of Dr. Shedd of that

Mission; and the whole scheme was explained to the leading men of the "millet," and approved by them. Two hundred and fifty Russian officers were to be sent to organise the Assyrian forces, which were to form part of the Black Sea-Baghdad line. The assent of the Persian Government had been secured; though it was admitted that they might growl, in oriental style, while yielding gladly enough to *force majeure.* Money and munitions were to be sent as needed.

On the faith of this promise, the nation continued in arms, and made an advance from Urmi to Khoi to meet the expected succours, overcoming some opposition from a Persian force on the way. However, the succour never came, and the expeditionary force had to return to its original position.

Before long it became clear that, though the plan was excellent in itself, yet it had no touch with the facts of the case. That unprecedented fact in history, the utter collapse of the whole Russian Empire, gradually became undeniable, and men saw that it was no mere question of a wall that threatened to fall, and that might be held in position by a few buttresses, but rather a matter of the disintegration of the bricks that had made it, back into the original mud and slime from which they had been made. Russia had collapsed, and there could be no further question of help from her, while the British were far away in the south and seemingly out of reach.

The Persian authorities, who had made no complaint of the free use of their territory by the Entente so long as things seemed to be going even moderately well for that party, now took an air of high virtue and authority, and ordered the Assyrians to lay down their arms. Thus Ijal-el-mulk, that distinguished scion of Persian royalty to whom we have made allusion above, published a grandiose proclamation, declaring that "Mosul was absolutely impregnable – had not the British been hammering at that rock for a year without detaching a single chip from its surface? How could they hope to take it, when Mackensen Sahib was himself therein? Russia was gone for ever, and the British could not help; what remained for the Assyrians but to lay down their arms? – though they must clearly understand that in that case Persia could guarantee absolutely no protection to anybody." The Assyrians naturally declined to surrender their arms on the clear understanding that they were to be massacred if they did so; and Mar Shimun sent an explanatory letter to the Vali Ahd of Persia, and to Mukt-i-shems, Governor of Tabriz – a Persian gentleman of English education – explaining that he and his were merely refugees in Persian territory, who carried arms solely to protect themselves, and expressing regret for any untoward incidents that might have occurred during their stay. Meantime, the mental temperature rose in Urmi, until at last the extremely unstable mixture of incompatible elements there reached its "flash-point," and the inevitable explosion occurred. What set it going is unknown; but perhaps the only extraordinary thing is that a mixture of fanatical Shiahs, of armed Christians who were once their serfs, and of turbulent mountaineers, should have kept from one anothers' throats for so long. No doubt it was the Russian force that controlled them, and when once that was withdrawn, the outbreak was only a matter of a few days or weeks.

On February 16th, 1918, some trifle started an *emeute* – each side being of course convinced that the other had formed an elaborate massacre-plot – and there were two days of sharp fighting in the streets of the town. Finally the Mussalmans were utterly put down and the city remained for the moment under the government of the "Mutwa" or Council of the Christians, of which the Patriarch was the official head. The Patriarch had distinguished himself – to his credit be it said – by his efforts to keep the peace before the outbreak, and to save life during it. The Persian Government had had a lesson to the effect that the Assyrians, even if they were cut off from Russia, were yet a formidable enemy for the Persian to deal with unaided.

Impressed with this fact, the Government adopted other and more thoroughly oriental methods, and took to assassination. Mukht-i-shems, that cultured and thoroughly westernised Persian gentleman, had been already in communication with Simco Agha, and now sent a signed letter to that chief, telling him plainly that if only he could remove Mar Shimun, the Persian Government would esteem it good service done. They found Simco not averse to profiting by the hint, now that it was clear to his mind which side was going to be victor in the war. He sent a letter to Mar Shimun, who was then residing in Salmas, suggesting that they should meet at a certain village in that district – of course under full safe conduct, for they were already sworn allies – and discuss the new situation caused by the Russian *debacle*. It seemed the obvious thing to do, and the Patriarch, accordingly, agreed to meet with Simco at the village of Koni Shehr, and he drove with his brother David and several other friends to that rendezvous (February 25, 1918). There were some warnings that danger was in the air; *e.g.*, an Armenian who was in American employ as a relief agent was resident in the village, and was told by a Kurd, "there is no danger for *your* folk." He sent off his son with a verbal message of warning at once, but this was unhappily disregarded. As Mar Shimun entered the house for the conference, his brother pointed out to him a group of armed Kurds on the roof, with a question as to what those fellows wanted; but the Patriarch brushed the matter aside, saying, "They have just gone up to see things from there," and went into the house. Simco was most cordial at the conference; the usual ceremonial hospitality was given; the utmost respect was shown to "the religious head of Kurdistan," and an agreement and alliance between Assyrians and Kurds reached on all points discussed. At last the business was done, and Simco, courteous host to the last, conducted his guest to his carriage, kissed his hand, Judas-like, in courtesy, and turned back into the house. That act was the signal; next instant there was one shot, and then a volley from the men previously posted on the roof, and the Patriarch lay dead in his carriage, a victim to his trust in the honour of a Kurd. It had been intended to massacre the whole party, and how the scheme miscarried is not known. The fact remains that Mar Shimun was the only important victim, though several of his following were killed; and how the Kurds failed to secure the life of his brother, David, is a mystery to this day. Somehow he found refuge in the house of an Armenian woman, who sheltered him during the search made for him that night, and showed him a way out of the town in the morning.

The Patriarch's body was treated with gross indignity, being set up for mockery in a sham "diwan," stripped, and flung out into the streets; but it was at last taken up by the Armenians of the place, and they, under the leadership of their priest, gave it honourable burial in their own church, where it lies to this day.

CHAPTER III

MIGRATION TO BRITISH PROTECTION

Assyrians were not likely to remain quiescent under such provocation as this, and almost as soon as the news of the murder of their Patriarch had reached Urmi, a force was despatched to revenge him, under his brother David, that Khoshaba of Tiari whom we have referred to above as one of the heroes of the mountain fighting, and another leader who now began to come to the front, Petros of Baz, who was usually known by the Kurdish title of Agha Petros.

Petros' previous career had been, we must regretfully own, picturesque rather than respectable, in that he, like some others of his nation, had laboured under invincible ignorance of one or two of the ten commandments; still, there is no doubt that the man is a born leader of irregular troops, and he became the general of his nation in the latter stages of the war. Under his leadership, Simco was utterly defeated, and his castle at Chara in the Salmas district was captured; though the Agha himself unfortunately escaped to be a thorn in the side of decency and order for a long time to come.

Still, his castle was secured, and with it the most private papers of its owner, including the letter of the Governor of Tabriz suggesting the murder of the Patriarch. One can hardly be surprised if the Assyrians felt, on pursuing it, that any understanding with the Persian Government was impossible, when its highest officials adopted this line of policy as a matter of course.

The position of the nation was now (March, 1918) very serious. They were in effect in possession of Urmi and the district to the north and south of that town, and they had a very fair supply of munitions, other than artillery, from the Russian arsenals; but they were cut off from all support, and had to reckon with the open hostility of Kurd, Persian and Turk, and with the secret enmity of all the Mussalman population of the town. However, fighting to the last in the hope of help either from north or south was the only possible policy, and regiments were enrolled and organised with that object. English help might perhaps arrive from the south, some day; but there was a vague chance of earlier assistance from the north: not indeed from the Russians, who had collapsed utterly, but from one of the Armenian parties.

Had the Armenians been united, this hope might have been almost a certainty; but division, that eternal curse of the oriental Christian, was rife among them, and the results were, as usual, fatal. Had they been united, then even without Russian support they might have defended Armenia against any force that the Turk was then in a position to send against them; but in fact the Armenians of the Caucasus were at open war with those of

Turkey, and the former were clamouring for peace with the Central Powers, and were deeply tainted with Bolshevism. To make confusion worse confounded, another line of division, even deeper than the other, cut across the original line of fissure; this was the renewal of the old quarrel between the two Armenian revolutionary societies, the "Tashnak" and the "Huntchak," which had been working for a time in partnership. Thus Andranik, who was the most skilful leader of the Armenians in the Van district, found himself first abandoned by the Russians; and when he attempted to make head against the Turk with Armenian troops only, the Russian Armenians abandoned him in the face of the enemy, and betrayed his plans to the Turks; while to crown all, the Tashnakists sought to murder him on the field of battle.

Under these circumstances the Turkish army advanced to Erzerum, and recaptured that important place without any opposition, except from what they described as "a few brigands"; and on entry they found themselves provided with absolutely everything that an army can require in the way of guns, rifles, ammunition, transport, and supply; all of which the Entente had forwarded to Russia for the Russian advance, and which was now abandoned to the enemy by those whom it had been intended to benefit. The Turks who entered the Caucasus were better provided than their army had ever been at any stage of the war.

Andranik had a personal following of about five thousand men, and with these he struck to the south, hoping to join with the Assyrians in Urmi – where Agha Petros was now in full command – and so present a front to the enemy. Given better co-ordination, it is probable that the plan might have succeeded and had important consequences; but Petros and Andranik, though both were excellent fighters and good guerrilla leaders, were neither of them real generals in a military sense, and they encountered in their Turkish opponent, Ali Ihsan Bey, one of the few Turks who showed real capacity during the war. Further, Petros had not the power of maintaining strict discipline among his wild army, though it must be owned that the Armenian seems to have had that gift in abundance.[9]

Thus when Andranik started to fight his way south to Urmi, the Turks, who held the interior lines, were able to prevent the junction. The Christian commanders had planned to meet between Salmas and Khoi, but the Assyrian advance to Salmas was checked, and Petros fell back, just at the time when a resolute advance would have found the Turks necessarily

---

[9] Andranik kept his men in the sternest order, and has been seen by an American witness to strike down a fellow convicted of looting, and literally stamp the life out of him with his heavy boots. Nevertheless, his men worshipped him, and followed him to the end, keeping up their coherence as a military body till the armistice at least. Like many good military leaders, he is a poor politician. As the whole of the Caucasus is full of abandoned military material he had no difficulty in providing his small force with all that it stood in need of.

withdrawing to meet the advance of Andranik and his Armenians on Khoi. Ali Ihsan turned back, being now free to meet his other opponent, and defeated him after desperate street fighting at Khoi itself. His victory was largely owing to the fact that Andranik (unable to restrain his own fighting ardour) plunged into the *melee* in the town, and so left his troops practically leaderless just when the eye of a general was needed to meet and defeat an outflanking movement of his enemies.

The Turks remained victorious, and another great attempt to put the Assyrian nation in touch with outside help had failed. Andranik never renewed his attempt, but withdrew on Julfa and the Caucasus, where he remained till the end of the war.

The courage of the Assyrians, however, was far from being broken, and indeed they were soon to win, under Petros' able leadership, successes more striking than any they had won yet. For three months they kept the field against a confederacy of Turks, Persians and Kurds, beating off a series of attacks, both to the north and south of Urmi. In one of these battles fought near Ushnu, they had the satisfaction of capturing 325 prisoners of the Turkish regular army, besides a large number of Kurdish tribesmen. Twenty-four of these prisoners were officers, and five machine-guns and two field guns were also among the spoils of war. The Assyrians, to their credit be it said, treated all their regular prisoners well, and released them within a very few days.[10] This is the more remarkable, as they were under very little discipline, and could not have been ignorant of the treatment being meted out by those Turkish officers to such villagers (let alone combatants) as fell into their hands.

To take an instance; the Turkish commander in Salmas at this time was Jevdet Bey, previously Vali of Van. (Ali Ihsan had been removed to the Mesopotamian front.) On one occasion this man forced the inhabitants of a village to dig a deep ditch at the foot of a high mud wall. When the ditch was completed, he marched the whole population, men, women and children, to the number, it is said, of seven hundred, down into the grave they had been forced to dig with their own hands; and then at a signal the wall (which had been previously undermined) was precipitated on them by soldiery posted on the further side of it, and the whole population of the village was buried alive. The sole excuse Jevdet ever alleged for his conduct was this, that he thought there was a plot among these people against his life.

On another occasion, the inhabitants of a second village, numbering about five hundred, were forced to surrender to the Kurds who surrounded them, after they had fired their last carriage. Terms of surrender were agreed to, and sworn to on the

---

[10] This chivalrous treatment was not, however, extended to Kurds at this period of the war, whatever may have been the case earlier. The writer questioned an Assyrian friend on the point and was informed, "After the murder of Mar Shimun we took no Kurdish prisoners." Quis condemnabit?

Koran, to the effect that all arms must be surrendered, but that life should be spared, and all allowed to depart in safety to Urmi. The arms were given up, and immediately the men were penned in one place, and the women in another. Every male was massacred forthwith, and every female between the ages of six and eighty was ravished, and then turned out naked to make her way to Urmi, two days' journey away.

Those who spared their enemies when those recollections were fresh, were at least not shaming their Christian name.

The fighting continued with varying fortunes, but on the whole the Christians held their own well, even though they lost some of the outlying districts. Isolated as the Assyrians were, however, they could not hope to do more than repulse their enemies. Further, their military stores were limited, though not their food; and every victory brought the exhaustion point nearer. Ammunition soon began to run perilously low, particularly as economy in the use of it is one of the last things that irregular troops can learn. Indeed, the end – which was nothing less than absolute national destruction – was actually in sight, and the position seemed absolutely hopeless, when on July 8, 1918, a veritable *deus ex machina* appeared to save the situation.

This was a British aeroplane, piloted by Capt. Pennington, who had achieved a flight daring even in the records of that corps to bring encouragement to those whom England, alone among their friends, had not quite forgotten. Starting from Miani, fully 150 miles to the south, he had undertaken to fly over unknown and hostile country to find an uncertain landing-place at the end of it, and arrived over Urmi to find a fresh danger awaiting him there. It was believed that his aeroplane was Turkish, and a heavy fire from all manner of weapons was opened upon him as he circled over the town looking for a landing. Ultimately, the meaning of the three circles of red, white and blue upon his wings became clear to the firing parties, and he landed in a field, to find that he had escaped the bullets only to run a further risk of death from suffocation, from the crowd who pressed upon him to kiss him.

One point must not be omitted. The airman, like many of his kind, was wearing "shorts" remarkable for their brevity. The ladies of Urmi felt that he must have met with some disaster to his garments, and begged to be allowed the honour of making the hero a pair of trousers!

Oriental-like, the men of Urmi thought their relief already assured by the coming of the aeroplane, but as a matter of fact, Captain Pennington had brought little but a message of hope. A few cavalry had been pushed up, far from their base in the neighbourhood of Baghdad, to see if anything could be done to help the Assyrians; and the flying-man was no more than a far advanced scout of this flying column in the wilderness. Captain

Pennington, however, had brought at least a coherent plan of action with him. If the Assyrians could hold on at Urmi, then officers, munitions and money would be sent to enable them to do so, and a first instalment of all three of these were now ready at Sain Kaleh, about 100 miles to the south.

The question was, how touch could be established, for Urmi was then threatened by a force of two Turkish divisions, the 5th and the 6th (stationed respectively to the north and south of the town), besides a considerable number of Persian and Kurdish irregulars. The obvious thing was for the "Urmi division" of Petros Agha's force to march to the south, break its way through the 6th division of the Ottomans at Saj Bulak, and then "contain them" with the bulk of the army, while a detachment was sent on to Sain Kaleh to bring in the promised supplies. The British force at Sain Kaleh consisted of no more than a squadron of cavalry (the 14th Hussars) and a machine-gun company, and could hardly be expected to force its way in alone. In fact, it had orders not to go beyond the point it had reached.

This then was the plan, the outlines of which were dictated in a letter brought by Captain Pennington, and the details discussed between that officer and Petros; it was adopted, and the airman departed on his return, it being then July 9th. The Assyrian detachment was to meet the English at Sain Kaleh on the 23rd of the month.

Up to a certain point, all was well, but in the later stages of this operation, all went awry, owing to two of the unfortunate characteristics of the nation concerned, viz., their inability to submit to discipline, and their ingrained suspiciousness of one another and every one else.

Petros marched out with the Urmi division of his army, leaving what was known as the Salmas division to guard his northern front. With his usual skill and daring, he completely defeated the Turkish division at Saj Bulak, and forced it to retreat to the hills near Rowanduz. Had he only left the bulk of his force to "contain" this defeated enemy and keep touch with Urmi, all might have gone well, but neither he nor his could resist the temptation of a triumphal march to greet the British at Sain Kaleh, and an equally triumphant return. Accordingly, they marched gaily on, quite untroubled by the facts that they were already some days late for their rendezvous (for time is nothing to an oriental) and that their latest enemy if defeated was not annihilated – and was left in their rear.

Meantime, things developed at Urmi rapidly and undesirably. The Turkish fifth division to the north of the town, hearing of the departure of a considerable part of the hostile force, commenced a formidable attack on their immediate opponents, the "Salmas division," and these fought with much less than their usual dash, declaring that they, being mountaineers, saw no reason to fight to the last for Urmi folk, now that "Petros had abandoned them and gone off to safety." The line of the Nazlu river which they had been ordered to hold, was lost, and the force fell back to the city.

Immediately, a general panic ensued, and the whole Christian population decided to do just the very last thing that the British commander had desired, viz., to evacuate the city and pour down the southern road to Sain Kaleh.

It may be dimly imagined what this resolution implied. Anything between fifty and seventy thousand men, women and children were started, without the least shadow of arrangement or discipline, on a march of rather over a hundred miles. It is true that most of them were able to provide their own transport; and as every oriental family is accustomed to store food for the whole year at harvest time (and the harvest was just in), most were able to provide themselves with food; so that had the way been unmolested, most would have accomplished the journey without too much difficulty. But the way was very far from being unmolested. There was, as has been said, no discipline in the body, and while it is not quite fair to say that on this great trek it was a case of "every man for himself and the devil (or Kurd) take the hindmost," yet it cannot be denied that it was a case of "each tribe for itself." There is little sense of national duty in the whole nation, though the mountaineers do recognise a sense of obligation to their own village, or tribe. They are still, as those who know them best have to recognise, in that stage in which our own Highlanders were some three hundred years ago; when they could be gathered for an attack on a common enemy, but not subjected to discipline, and when it meant nothing to Cameron or Stewart that MacDonalds of Glencoe were massacred by an opponent who was equally dangerous to them.

Thus, when tried by conditions that might have tested a disciplined army, the Assyrian organisation went to pieces, and the national trek became a wild rush for safety, a safety that could only have been attained by a resolute defence where they were.

Naturally, their opponents were on their track at once. The Kurds of the mountains, and the Persians of Urmi, came down upon them like wolves upon a herd of cattle, and there was a hundred miles of plunder and massacre, in which no mercy was shown. Men were slaughtered, women stripped and violated, girls carried off to Mussalman harems; fully a fourth of the whole nation must have perished in those terrible days. It was the plainsmen who suffered most, for the conditions were more familiar to the mountaineers, who were used to trek and battle, and who acted better together.

The men of Tiari, for instance, not only brought their own women through safely, but even their sheep as well, as they had done on their previous migration. It was a sign that they at least did not lose military cohesion on this occasion either. It is said, unkindly but plausibly, that they even arrived at the end of the journey with more sheep than they had at the beginning of it, having "collected" the balance from hostile villages on the road!

While this was going on at Urmi, Petros and his force had reached Sain Kaleh, on July 30, quite undisturbed in their oriental minds at the fact that they were eight days at least behind the time that they had themselves fixed for the rendezvous. The little British force had waited several days beyond the time, at the most extreme risk, but had at last felt itself obliged to commence its own retreat to the south, so that the Assyrians on their arrival were surprised to find nobody there. However, the British were only one day to the south, and the junction was duly effected, and preparations made to hand over the supplies as arranged; when the amazing news of the evacuation of Urmi, and of the arrival of hordes of disorganised and needy refugees at Sain Kaleh, reached the British commander. Instantly he and his force returned to that point (August 3rd), to find the matter even worse than they had expected. Thousands had been massacred on the road, partly by the Persians, under that Mejid-es-Sultaneh who has been referred to earlier in this narrative, partly by the Turkish 6th division, which had returned from Rowanduz in order to revenge their defeat upon these helpless fugitives. More than fifty thousand remained, however, and these were now pouring in to

Sain Kaleh to fling themselves on British protection and charity; while the Kurds and Persians were on their track certain that they could now get revenge and plunder to their hearts' content. But on their arrival at that point, the Kurds found the British once more in occupation of it, and a squadron of cavalry and a machine-gun company were different game from a horde of women and unarmed men. Nevertheless, the Mussalmans were not disposed to give up their prospects without a snap at least, and their leader, Mejid-es-Sultaneh, whatever his record in other respects, is at least a brave man. Hence there were three days of sharp fighting while the cavalry covered the passage of the refugees, who were still arriving in streams; and it was at this time that a daring feat was performed that merits record. A strong force of Kurds was harrying a number of refugees, when a party of British soldiers (three officers and four B.O.R.'s) appeared upon the scene. For seven men to attack several hundred would seem to be facing hopeless odds, but these men without hesitation dashed into the midst of the Kurds with a Lewis gun upon their saddles, and dismounting, opened such a fire as to put the Kurds to flight in all that part of the field. The leader, Captain Savage, secured a well-earned D.S.O. for the feat, and one of his companions, Captain Scott Ollson, was awarded the Military Cross.

Ultimately, the Kurds and Turks withdrew,[11] abandoning their prey, and the question had now to be faced of what was to be done with the refugees. To leave them to perish was impossible, and it was decided to march them to Hamadan and Kirmanshah, where they would be within reach of the protection of the British, and this decision was carried out. The march was no easy one, and of course no supplies had been provided for the unexpected multitude of refugees. It must be frankly admitted that the Assyrians plundered right and left. There certainly was every excuse for them, for they were a starving crowd of armed men, who had lost their all at the hands of these Mussalmans, who had proclaimed the "Jehad" against them; and they now thought themselves entitled to "get their own back" as they had the opportunity. Probably the men of any race would have done the same under like circumstances, even had they not been brought up, like most of these mountaineers, to consider an open raid a totally different thing from stealing by stealth. There is, moreover, one thing that must be mentioned to their credit. We have seen what sort of recollections were fresh in their minds about the treatment of such women of theirs as had fallen into the hands of their enemies. Now it was their turn, and Mussalman villages by the score lay at their mercy as they marched through the land; yet

---

[11] One very valuable life was sacrificed at Sain Kaleh. Dr. Shedd, the American missionary, who had shared the sufferings of the people throughout, died of typhus at that place.

in no single instance was there even complaint that a Mussalman woman had met with insult or maltreatment at Christian hands.

Finally, the emigrating nation reached Hamadan, where the irregular levies they had formed were taken under the control of British officers; a decision that caused great satisfaction to most of them, but yet great grief to a certain Amazon lady, who had hitherto acted as commander of the group of some thirty men who came from her own village in the land of Berwar. The lady in question, whose name is Tabriz,[12] had led her contingent in more than one fight, and kept them in full order on the march with the help of a heavy whip which she wielded most unhesitatingly. Riding astride of her horse, with rifle at back and revolver at hip, she had been a most efficient officer, while the fact that she was the sister or cousin of the bishop of her district had lent her local prestige. Now she had to hand over her command to a mere man, for British officers, though accustomed to much unusual material in the making of soldiery, are not yet educated to the point of employing Amazons. Her last prayer was to the effect that the twenty-five rifles which were the armament of her contingent might be returned to her at the conclusion of peace, and at least a receipt was given her for the coveted articles.

---

[12] Town names are often used as girls' names by Assyrians. Besides Tabriz, the writer is acquainted with "Tiflis" and "Romi" (Rome).

From Hamadan the nation was brought gradually down to Baquba, a point some thirty miles from Baghdad, and established in a city of tents at that point. It may be stated that the officers who now controlled the levies could not say enough in praise of the endurance and cheerfulness of the mountaineer battalion in the course of a very trying march, and that regiment was retained, at all events for the moment, in British service.[13]

At that place they remain at the date of writing, the guests of the British Government, and it has been the lot of another writer to describe what he rightly regards as one of the most picturesque episodes of the war, the establishment of a "Modern City of Refuge."[14] The question of their repatriation, and of their future lot, is one for later decision as well as later description, but we may express the hope that those who have suffered so much will return under British Protection to their own homes, where it may well be their destiny to be a useful element in the future development which, we hope, awaits turbulent and rugged

---

[13] This regiment has since been employed, to its own great content, in a small hill campaign against its old Kurdish enemies. It must be admitted that they were (to quote an eye-witness) "a little indiscriminate," and after they had finished dealing with the stronghold of an old enemy, one of their officers wrote gleefully to a friend, "Now you would not say that there ever had been a house there."
Still the General Officer under whom they served reported very highly of them, both as campaigners and as fighting men, declaring that they did fully as well as the picked Indian troops (Garwhalis) with whom they were brigaded.
[14] "A Modern City of Refuge!" by "Eye-Witness." Mesopotamian Correspondent of the *Pioneer*.

Kurdistan. Can Great Britain, now that she is responsible for order in the country, afford to neglect so valuable a military asset as this nation has proved itself to be?

www.ingramcontent.com/pod-product-compliance
Lightning Source LLC
LaVergne TN
LVHW051511070426
835507LV00022B/3059